Best 100 Calorie or Less Dessert Recipes

Diana Loera

Copyrighted 2014

All rights reserved. All content in this book is copyrighted and may not be shared or distributed without the written consent of Diana Loera and Loera Publishing LLC.

One example of the scrumptious 100 calorie or less dessert recipes that await you in this book

Additional Books by Diana Loera

I am always looking for cool recipes and interesting topics. Below are some of my books. More are being researched and written every month.

Thank you for your interest in my books!

Summertime Sangria

Best Copycat Recipes on the Planet

Party Time Chicken Wing Recipes

Awesome Thanksgiving Leftovers Revive Guide

Best Venison Recipes

Meet Me at the County Fair – Fair Food Recipes

What is the Paleo Diet & Paleo Diet Recipe Sampler

12 Extra Special Summer Dessert Fondue Recipes

14 Extra Special Winter Holidays Fondue Recipes

USA Based Wholesale Directory 2014

Fast Start Guide to Flea Market Selling

I601A – Our Journey to Ciudad Juarez

Stop Hot Flashes Now

Please visit www.LoeraPublishing.com to view all titles and descriptions. Thank you.

Introduction

Hello! Diana Loera here. Thank you for buying my book.

I am always on the lookout for cutting edge topics and cool recipes.

About three years ago, when I was, once again, shelling out money to buy overpriced prepackaged 100 calorie snacks I thought to myself that there has to be a cheaper way to have desserts that are 100 calories or less.

Plus. I was getting pretty burned out on selection, or lack thereof.

In this book I've compiled an assortment of 100 calorie recipes – some are even a few less calories. Desserts from chocolate glazed donuts to healthy cookies to cheesecakes and more. I've included a few of the popular mug cake recipes in hard to find 100 calorie versions too.

Not only are these tasty treats great for fast at home snacks but excellent for parties or showers too.

Due to past requests from those who have read my other recipe books, I like to include color photos. Please keep in mind the more photos that I add the more the printing cost increases so I am as selective as possible when adding photos.

I also publish all my books in 8 ½ by 11 format as personally, I hate squinting at small font and trying to follow instructions from a Lilliputian sized book.

I hope you enjoy making and trying these recipes as much as I have enjoyed making and sharing them with you.

Sincerely,

Diana

P.S. One recipe is 103 calories – it was one of those too good to not include recipes but I did want to let you know in advance. It is also listed in the recipe that it is 103 calories. There are some recipes under 90 calories too.

Imagine yourself enjoying decadent treats like this one – and knowing it was only a 100 calories or even less

Table of Contents

Additional Books by Diana Loera 3

Introduction 4

Chocolate Glazed Baked Chocolate Donuts 7

80 Calorie Skinny Cupcake 8

Chocolate Oatmeal Almond Butter Cookies 9

Fast and Easy No Bake Oatmeal Peanut Butter Cookies 10

Mini Berry Topped Cheesecakes 11

Chocolate Peanut Butter Brownies 12

Skinny Chocolate Peanut Butter Cup Shake 13

100 Calorie Chocolate Cake 14

To Be Shared Chocolate Cake 15

30-Second 100 Calorie Chocolate Cake 17

100 Calorie Chocolate Mug Cake 18

100 Calorie Single Serving Brownie 19

1-2-3 Mug Cake 20

100 Calorie Oat Bran Banana Protein Muffins, ... 21

Secretly Healthy 87 Calorie Brownies 23

Double Lemon Pudding Cookies 24

No-Bake Coconut Crazy Bars 25

Plain Jane Baked Vegan Doughnuts 26

Double Fudge Banana Muffins 28

Skinny Lemon Sunshine `Gingersnap Cheesecake Bars 29

100 Calorie Raspberry Chocolate Chip Protein Brownies 30

Chewy Raspberry Apple Granola Bars 33

Guilt Free Chocolate Soufflé 34

Chocolate Peanut Butter Brownies 35

Strawberry Banana Smoothie 37

103 Calorie Chocolate Cupcakes 38

Apple-Fig Compote 40
Thank You 42

Chocolate Glazed Baked Chocolate Donuts

Ingredients:

Donuts:
1 cup whole wheat pastry flour
1/4 cup unsweetened cocoa powder
1/4 cup sugar
1 Tbsp. baking powder
1/4 tsp salt
1 egg
1/2 cup almond milk
1 tsp vanilla
1 Tbsp. canola oil
3 Tbsp. unsweetened applesauce

Chocolate Glaze:
1/2 cup semisweet chocolate chips
1 tsp canola oil
1 Tbsp. corn syrup
1/4 tsp vanilla extract

Directions:

Preheat the oven to 450 degrees and coat a donut pan liberally with cooking spray.

Stir together flour, cocoa powder, sugar, baking powder, and salt in a large bowl. Add the egg, milk, vanilla, oil, and applesauce; stir together for 1 minute.

Fill each cavity in the pan 1/2 of the way full with batter. Bake for 7 to 8 minutes or until the donuts spring back when lightly touched. Cool completely.

Meanwhile, melt the chocolate in a microwave safe bowl. Add the corn syrup and oil and microwave in 20 second increments, stirring in between. Stir in the vanilla. Dunk each donut into the glaze and allow to set. Yield: 14 donuts.

Nutrition Information (per donut): 93 calories; 3.4 g. fat; 15 mg. cholesterol; 157 mg. sodium; 15.2 g. carbohydrate; 1.9 g. fiber; 1.1 g. protein

80 Calorie Skinny Cupcake

Total Time: 25 minutes
Calories per serving: 80

Ingredients:

1 cake mix
1 1/2 cups of Sprite Zero

Directions:

Preheat the oven to 350 degrees.

Combine the Sprite Zero and the cupcake in a bowl. Stir to combine

Pour in the cupcake pan to make 20 cupcakes.

Bake for 17-20 minutes or until they start to brown.

Allow to cool slightly. Serve as it or top with a little bit of powdered sugar so they look cute!

Chocolate Oatmeal Almond Butter Cookies

Ingredients:

1 cup Almond Butter, stirred well
1/4 cup Gluten Free Rolled Oats
1/4 cup Sucanat Sugar
1 large egg
3/4 tsp baking soda
1/2 tsp sea salt
3 oz. dark chocolate (try Lindt Extra Dark Chocolate 85% Cocoa), broken into small pieces

Directions:

1. Preheat oven to 350 degrees F.
2. In a medium bowl, combine the first six ingredients until blended. Stir in Chocolate.
3. Drop dough by rounded tablespoonful on to parchment lined baking sheets or non-stick baking sheets.
4. Bake for 10-12 minutes or until lightly browned.
5. Let cool for approximately five minutes on baking sheets. Remove to a wire rack and let cool for 15 more minutes.

Yields approximately 24 cookies.

Per Cookie
Calories: 75
Protein: 2g
Fat: 6g
Carbs: 5g

Fast and Easy No Bake Oatmeal Peanut Butter Cookies

Ingredients:

1/3 cup granulated sugar
2 teaspoons unsweetened cocoa
2 tablespoons fat free milk
2 tablespoons crunchy peanut butter
1/4 teaspoon vanilla
1/2 cup quick-cooking rolled oats

Directions:

Stir together sugar, cocoa and milk in 4-cup glass measure or medium microwave-safe bowl.

Microwave on high 1 to 1-1/4 minutes or until boiling, stirring once.

Stir in peanut butter and vanilla until blended. Stir in oats until combined.
Drop by the spoonful onto a waxed paper-lined plate to make 6 cookies.

Cool in freezer 10 minutes before serving.

Nutrition Information:

Serving Size 6 servings (1 cookie each)
Calories 100 per cookie

Mini Berry Topped Cheesecakes

Ingredients:

Fifteen 1 1/2 to 2-inch ginger snaps (Midel or other brand)
8 ounces Neufchatel cheese (see note)
1/2 cup 1% cottage cheese (no salt added)
2 large eggs
1/4 cup sugar
1 teaspoon vanilla extract
Raspberries, blackberries, blueberries for decorating
Special equipment: paper muffin tin liners

Directions:

Preheat to 325 F and place rack in center of oven. Line muffin tins with paper liners. Set one cookie into the bottom of each liner.

Put the Neufchatel cheese, cottage cheese, eggs, sugar, and vanilla into a large bowl and use a beater to mix until smooth, with no obvious lumps remaining from the cottage cheese.

Spoon 2 tablespoons of batter into each muffin tin.

Bake until the cheesecakes are just firm in the center, 10-12 minutes.

Remove from oven and chill. Decorate with berries just before serving.

Note: Neufchatel cheese is similar in taste and texture to cream cheese, although naturally has about 1/3 of the fat.

Each mini cheesecake is 100 calories.

Chocolate Peanut Butter Brownies

Ingredients:

5 egg whites
1.5 scoops chocolate protein powder (we used Trutein Chocolate Peanut Butter Cup)
3/4 cup pumpkin
1/4 cup unsweetened cocoa powder (Hershey's Special Dark works best here)
2 tbsp. coconut flour
2 tbsp. powdered peanut butter + 3 tbsp. for peanut butter swirl (we used PB2)**
1/4 cup mini semi-sweet chocolate chips
1 tsp vanilla
1/2 tsp baking soda
3/4 tsp apple cider vinegar*
Stevia to taste

* do not omit as this helps keep the brownies light and fluffy! **

You can also substitute real peanut butter for the powdered peanut butter. Just microwave the peanut butter for about 20 seconds, stir and drizzle on cupcakes. Note that this will change the nutritional information.

Directions:

Preheat oven to at 350 and spray a 9 x 9 baking pan with nonstick spray. In a medium sized bowl, beat egg whites with an electronic mixer for about 30 seconds or until egg whites are "foamy," then add all of your wet ingredients and mix well by hand. Set bowl aside. In another bowl, combine all dry ingredients except for the chocolate chips. Slowly add your dry ingredients into your wet ingredients and mix well by hand, then fold in the chocolate chips. Pour batter into your prepared pan. To make the peanut butter swirl: In a small bowl add 3 tbsp. of powdered peanut butter and approximately 1.5 tbsp. of water and mix well (you may need more or less water, but you need a slightly "runny" peanut butter). Drizzle the peanut butter over the brownie batter. Then, using a knife gently swirl the batters together. Bake at 350 for 20-25 minutes.

Calories: 92
Fat: 3.2 g
Carbs: 8.7 g
Fiber: 2.6 g
Protein: 8.7 g
WW Points +: 2 pts

Skinny Chocolate Peanut Butter Cup Shake

Ingredients:

¾ cup unsweetened almond milk, frozen (6 cubes)
¾ cup unsweetened almond milk
1 Tbs. unsweetened cocoa powder (I use Scharffen Berger)
1 Tbs. original PB2 powder
1 Tbs. Splenda

Directions:

Place all of the ingredients into a high speed blender and blend until smooth. Pour into a tall glass and enjoy.

100 calories

100 Calorie Chocolate Cake

Ingredients:

1 gluten free flour or regular white flour
6 tbsp. cacao or unsweetened cocoa powder (30g)
1/2 tsp baking soda
1/2 tsp salt
3/4 cup xylitol or granulated sugar of choice (140g)
1/2 cup mini chocolate chips, optional
1/4 cup yogurt of choice (such as Wholesoy) (60g)
3/4 cup water (180g)
1/4 cup almond butter, peanut butter, or allergy-friendly alternative (60g)
2 tsp pure vanilla extract (8g)

Instructions:

Preheat oven to 350 degrees F, and grease an 8-in square or round pan. Set aside. In a large bowl, combine the flour, cocoa powder, baking soda, salt, optional chips, and sweetener, and stir very well. (If your nut butter is not stir-able, gently heat it until stir-able.) In a new bowl, whisk together the nut butter, yogurt, water, and vanilla. Pour wet into dry and stir until just combined (don't over-mix), then pour into the greased pan. Bake 25 minutes or until batter has risen and a toothpick inserted into the center of the cake comes out mostly clean. (I like to take it out when it's still a little undercooked, let it cool, and then set in the fridge overnight. This prevents overcooking, and the cake will still firm up nicely as it sits.)
If you can wait, I highly recommend not taking a taste until the next day. This cake is so much richer and sweeter after sitting for a day.

Calories: 95

To Be Shared Chocolate Cake

Prep time: 5 minutes
Cook time: 15 minutes
Total time: 20 minutes

Makes one larger size personal cake or two normal portions for just 100 calories.

Ingredients

2 tablespoons Cacao Powder (or normal cocoa)
3 tablespoons GF Oat Flour
3 tablespoons Almond Milk (or nondairy milk of choice)
1 Egg White (or 3 tablespoons Liquid Egg Whites)
2 teaspoons Coconut Oil
½ tsp pure Vanilla Extract
2 tablespoons Baking Stevia
½ tsp Baking Powder
⅛ Tsp Sea Salt
Optional: Any desired additional flavors such as chocolate chips, peanut butter, mint extract (or other extracts), coconut but remember, any additions will change the calorie count.

Instructions

Preheat oven to 350 degrees Fahrenheit
Combine all dry ingredients in a bowl
Add all wet ingredients and mix until combined
Pour cake batter into 1 cup ramekin sprayed with nonstick spray (can also make two ½-cup ramekins for two!)
Bake in oven for 12-14 minutes, being careful not to over bake
Drizzle/Top with melted chocolate or any other desired toppings

Notes
Only 200 calories for a single cake with 8 grams of protein, or make it into two ½ cup ramekins and create two 100 calorie portions.

Nutrition Information
Serving size: 1
Calories: 220
Sugar: 1.2
Protein: 8

30-Second 100 Calorie Chocolate Cake

Ingredients:

2 tbsp. flour
1 1/2 tbsp. no-calorie sweetener
2 tsp. cocoa powder
1/4 tsp. baking powder
Pinch of salt
2 tbsp. milk
1 tsp. oil
1 drop of vanilla extract

Directions:

Spray a mug or ramekin with cooking spray. In the cup combine the flour, sweetener, cocoa powder, baking powder, and salt until no lumps remain. Stir in the milk, olive oil, and vanilla until smooth.

Cook in the microwave on high for 30 seconds. You may need to add 5-10 more seconds depending on your microwave.
Note: don't overcook or it will be rubbery. It should be moist on the bottom and will continue cooking as it sets.

I like to add a sprinkle of powdered sugar, but you could top it with fruit or whipped cream – just remember that additions change the calorie count.

Adding a cherry garnish adds a nice finish to this mug cake

100 Calorie Chocolate Mug Cake

Ingredients

2 tablespoons self-rising flour
2 tablespoons cocoa powder
3 tablespoons stevia for baking
2 tablespoons unsweetened apple sauce
2 tablespoons 35 calorie per serving unsweetened almond milk
1 egg white

Instructions

Add all ingredients to a large mug. Whisk well with a fork.

Microwave on high for 2 minutes.

100 Calorie Single Serving Brownie

Ingredients

1 tablespoon flour
1 tablespoon sugar
1 tablespoon cocoa powder
2 tablespoons of apple sauce
Pinch of baking soda
Pinch of salt

Instructions

Mix all the ingredients together in a mug
Put in microwave for 1-1:15 minutes.
Put a little bit of powdered sugar on top.
Enjoy

Notes
If you want it a little creamier, add a teaspoon of Nutella. Just remember it does increase the calorie count but I think you'll find it may be worth it occasionally

1-2-3 Mug Cake

Ingredients:

1 box Angel Food cake mix
1 box any flavor cake mix
2 T. water

Directions:

Using a large plastic bowl with a tightly fitting lid or a large zip lock bag, combine the two boxes of cake mix stirring or shaking well.

For each individual serving, take out 3 Tablespoons of the cake mixture and mix it with 2 Tablespoons of water in a small microwave safe container. I used a small coffee mug. Microwave on high for 1 minute. You now have your own instant individual cake and it is warm and inviting. You can top with a dollop of fruit or whipped topping if you like but just remember any additions will increase the calorie count.

Try various flavors of cake mix but it must always be combined with an Angel Food mix.

Keep the mix tightly sealed in an airtight container until used and remember: This recipe is called 1-2-3 Cake because all you need to remember is 3 Tablespoons mix, 2 Tablespoons water, and 1 minute in the microwave.

If you keep one recipe on hand, this is the one I would choose as once you create the mix in the zip lock bag, you can whip these tasty cakes up in a couple minutes and offset any higher calorie snacking fast.

You can even portion this out into a small zip lock bag and take to work for a fast tasty treat versus high calorie vending machine junk.

I garnished the one in the photo with a pinch of coconut but remember, to do so sparingly and also remember that any addition will increase your calorie count.

1 2 3 Mug Cake

100 Calorie Oat Bran Banana Protein Muffins,

Prep Time: 5 minutes
Cook Time: 15 minutes
Total Time: 20 minutes

Ingredients:

1 2/3 cup oat bran
1 scoop vanilla protein powder
1 tablespoon baking powder
1/4 teaspoon baking soda
1 teaspoon cinnamon
2 small or medium very ripe bananas, mashed
1/2 cup unsweetened applesauce
1/2 cup nonfat plain Greek yogurt
2 large egg whites
1 teaspoon vanilla extract

Instructions:

Preheat oven to 400 degrees F. Spray 12 cup muffin tin with nonstick cooking spray or grease well with coconut oil

In a medium bowl, whisk together oat bran, protein powder, baking powder, baking soda, and cinnamon; then set aside

In a large bowl, mix mashed banana, applesauce, Greek yogurt, egg whites, and vanilla together until well combined and smooth. Add wet ingredients to dry ingredients and mix until just combined. Let batter sit two minutes to thicken a bit. Divide batter evenly into 12 muffin cups and bake 15 minutes or until toothpick inserted into center comes out clean. Transfer to a wire rack to cool for 10 minutes, then remove muffins from tin and place on wire rack to cool completely.

Nutrition Information:

Serving size: 1 muffin
Calories: 95
Fat: 1.4g
Carbohydrates: 17.3g
Sugar: 4.5 g
Fiber: 3.3g
Protein: 6.3g

Enjoy tasty muffins that you won't believe are only 95 calories

If under 100 calories doesn't impress you- check out how many calories are in these muffins
http://www.dunkindonuts.com/content/dunkindonuts/en/menu/food/bakery/muffins/muffins.html?DRP_FLAVOR=Blueberry

or the calorie counts in these treats

http://www.starbucks.com/menu/catalog/nutrition?food=all#view_control=nutrition

Secretly Healthy 87 Calorie Brownies

Calories are calculated for cutting the amount into 15 bars (not counting the optional add-ins). So you are enjoying one brownie with less than 100 calories and it is a good for you brownie too.

Ingredients:

2 cups finely grated zucchini (firmly packed)
1 cup brown sugar
1 1/3 cup applesauce (unsweetened)
2 eggs
2 teaspoons vanilla
2/3 cup flour
1 cup cocoa powder
2 teaspoons baking soda
1 1/2 teaspoons baking powder
1/2 teaspoon cinnamon
1/2 teaspoon salt

Optional add-ins- just remember that these will increase the calorie count
Cup of chocolate chips and/or nuts
Frosting: 1/2 cup chocolate chips, 1/2 cup butterscotch chips, and 1/2 cup peanut butter melted together

Directions:

Preheat the oven to 350°F. Grease a 9x13 inch pan.
Mix together the zucchini, sugar, applesauce, eggs, and vanilla.

Stir together the remaining ingredients and add to the wet ingredients, stirring until combined.

Stir in the chocolate chips and/or nuts if using.

Bake for about 55 minutes.

Allow to cool and then use the optional frosting.

Double Lemon Pudding Cookies

Ingredients:

1 ¾ cup all-purpose flour
1 ½ tsp baking powder
¼ tsp salt
1 tbsp. lemon zest
4 tbsp. unsalted butter, melted and cooled
2 large eggs, room temperature
1 tbsp. vanilla extract
¾ c + 2 tbsp. granulated sugar
1 (1 oz.) box sugar-free, fat-free lemon pudding mix – remember – Sugar Free mix

Instructions

Preheat the oven to 350°F, and line two baking sheets with parchment paper or Silpats.

In a medium bowl, whisk together the flour, baking powder, salt, and zest. In a separate bowl, whisk together the butter, eggs, and vanilla. Add in the sugar, mixing until thoroughly incorporated. Stir in the pudding mix. Add in the flour mixture, stirring just until incorporated.

(Optional: Chill for 30 minutes for thicker cookies that do not spread during baking.)

Drop the cookie dough into 22 rounded scoops onto the prepared baking sheets. (If the cookie dough was chilled, flatten slightly.) Bake at 350°F for 10-11 minutes. Cool on the pan for 10 minutes before turning out onto a wire rack.

Calories: 98 per serving

No-Bake Coconut Crazy Bars

Ingredients

1 cup shredded coconut (unsweetened) (80g)
1/4 cup agave or pure maple syrup
2 tbsp. virgin coconut oil
1/2 tsp pure vanilla extract
1/8 tsp salt

Instructions

Combine all ingredients in a food processor or mix thoroughly by hand. Firmly pack into a small container – 7 x 5 is the size I used.
Place in refrigerator for 30 – 40 minutes.
Cut into even sized bars – using a 7x5 cut evenly, each bar will be about 100 calories.

Per Bar:

Calories: 100
Fat: 8g
Carbs: 7g
Protein: 1.5g
Fiber: 1.5g
WW Points (new system): 3

Plain Jane Baked Vegan Donuts

Don't turn your nose up at this Plain Jane recipe. It may not sound as decadent as some of the other recipes in this book but these donuts make a perfect morning on the go treat.

Dry Ingredients. I

1 Cup All Purpose Flour
1/2 Cup Sugar (I use raw cane sugar, you could use white sugar)
1 1/2 tsp Baking Powder
1/4 tsp Salt
1/4 tsp Nutmeg
1/4 tsp Cinnamon

Wet Ingredients

1/2 Cup Soymilk (I like vanilla flavored unsweetened)
1/2 tsp Apple Cider Vinegar (
1/2 tsp Pure Vanilla Extract
Egg Replacer for 1 Egg (If you don't use egg replacer use 1 egg)
4 Tablespoons butter

Icing Glaze:
1/2 cup powdered sugar
1 Tablespoon soy milk

Directions:

Preheat oven to 350F.
Take all the wet ingredients and put in a small pot on the stovetop on low. Whisk ingredients together to blend well.
Do not let the mixture get too hot, it should be just warm to the touch.
Mix the dry ingredients together in a large bowl.
Add the wet to the dry and mix until just incorporated.
Do not over mix. The batter will be very sticky.

Carefully put the sticky dough in the doughnut pan one tablespoon at a time.

Bake for 12 minutes.

You don't want the doughnuts to become dark brown, they should slowly pop up when pressed with a finger.

Cool on a wire rack and then frost

Makes 20 mini doughnuts.

Calories: 78

Double Fudge Banana Muffins

Ingredients:

1 egg
1/4 cup brown sugar
1/3 cup applesauce (unsweetened)
1 teaspoon vanilla
1 cup mashed bananas (about 3 bananas)
1 cup oat flour (or substitute all-purpose flour)
1/2 teaspoon baking soda
1/2 teaspoon baking powder
1/2 teaspoon salt
1/4 cup cocoa powder
Chocolate chips (optional- which will drive your calories up)

Instructions:

Preheat oven to 350ºF.
Grease muffin tin (the recipe makes 10 regular sized muffins or 5 in a big muffin tin).
Whisk together the egg, sugar, applesauce, vanilla, and bananas.
Mix the dry ingredients and add to the wet.
Mix just until combined.
Bake for about 20-25 minutes for regular muffins or 25-30 minutes for big muffins

Skinny Lemon Sunshine `Gingersnap Cheesecake Bars

I love gingersnaps and I love lemon – the marriage of these two flavors brings a burst of summer sunshine to your mouth.   Be sure to place any leftovers in the fridge – they should keep okay for up to 4 – 5 days.

Ingredients:

Crust
1 ¼ c gingersnap smashed to crumb size
1 Tbsp. unsalted butter, melted
2 Tbsp. unsweetened applesauce

For the filling
2 (8 oz.) blocks fat-free cream cheese, softened
½ c granulated sugar
1 tbsp. lemon zest
1 egg white
2 tsp all-purpose flour
2 tsp vanilla extract
1 tbsp. lemon juice

Instructions:

Preheat the oven to 300°F, and lightly coat an 8"-square baking pan with nonstick cooking spray. To prepare the crust, stir together the gingersnap crumbs, butter, and applesauce. Press evenly into the bottom of the prepared pan, and bake at 300°F for 6 minutes. Cool on a wire rack. While the crust bakes, prepared the filling. Add the cream cheese, sugar, and lemon zest to a medium bowl, and beat until smooth. Add the egg white, flour, vanilla, and lemon juice, and beat until thoroughly incorporated. Spread on top of the cooled crust.
Bake at 300°F for 28-33 minutes, or until the center barely jiggles when gently shaken. Cool completely to room temperature before covering the top with plastic wrap, ensuring that the plastic wrap completely touches the entire surface of the cheesecake. Chill for at least 3 hours before slicing into squares.

100 Calorie Raspberry Chocolate Chip Protein Brownies

This recipe does take some time to make and you may need to gather ingredients that you normally don't have in your pantry. While I like the fast and easy recipes, I did want to include a few recipes like this one as it is a healthy and very tasty dessert. You can make a batch of these and take one bar with you daily to work for a tasty and healthy treat.

Prep time: 10 minutes
Cook time: 20 minutes
Total time: 30 minutes

Ingredients:

1/4 cup gluten free rolled oats
1/2 cup unsweetened cocoa powder
1/2 cup Whey Chocolate Protein Powder
1/2 cup unsweetened applesauce
1 egg
1 tablespoon honey
1 teaspoon vanilla extract
2/3 cup Blue Diamond Almond Breeze Unsweetened Vanilla or Chocolate Almond Milk
2 tablespoons coconut oil
1/4 cup chocolate chips, plus 2 tablespoons for topping
1/2 cup raspberries

Directions:

Preheat oven to 350 degrees F.
Spray 8x8 inch baking pan with nonstick cooking spray.
Place oats in blender and blend for a minute or until they resemble the consistency of flour (yes, you just made oat flour).
Transfer oat flour to medium bowl then whisk in protein powder and cocoa powder; set aside.
Whisk together applesauce, egg, honey, vanilla and almond milk until smooth and well combined.
Add to dry ingredients and mix together until just combined.
Heat coconut oil and 1/4 cup of the chocolate chips in a small saucepan over very low heat; stir continuously until all chocolate chips and coconut oil have melted together.

Gently stir into brownie batter.
Pour mixture into prepared pan. Sprinkle remaining 2 tablespoons of chocolate chips and raspberries on top or you can swirl them in the batter with a knife.
Bake for 18-22 minutes or until just cooked through and the top has set.
Transfer pan to wire rack to cool completely.
Once cool, cut into 12 bars -- please note that bars should be kept covered in the refrigerator and enjoyed chilled.

Notes:

This recipe used Pro Performance AMP Amplified Wheybolic Extreme 60 Chocolate Protein Powder from GNC and the calories reflect that each scoop is about 90 calories.

If you don't have unsweetened applesauce on hand, you can substitute with 1 small ripe banana.

Nutrition Information

Serving size: 1 brownie
Calories: 100
Fat: 5.5g Carbohydrates: 11.5g Sugar: 7g Fiber: 2g Protein: 5g

Chewy Raspberry Apple Granola Bars

While I love chocolate, sometimes I like something non chocolate and this was a really good change of pace.

Ingredients:

1 tsp coconut oil, melted
½ c unsweetened applesauce, room temperature
1/3 c skim milk
1 Tbsp. honey
1 tsp ground cinnamon
2 ½ c old-fashioned oats
1 cup frozen unsweetened raspberries, diced

Instructions:

Preheat the oven to 350°F, and lightly coat an 8"-square baking pan with nonstick cooking spray.
In a large bowl, stir together the oil and applesauce until smooth.
Mix in the milk, honey and cinnamon until thoroughly combined.
Stir in the oats until evenly coated with the applesauce mixture.
Gently fold in the raspberries.
Press the oat mixture into the prepared pan, and bake at 350°F for 16-19 minutes. Cool completely to room temperature in the pan before slicing into 10 bars.

It's important for the applesauce to be at room temperature to prevent the melted coconut oil from re-solidifying.

For best storage results, tightly wrap each individual bar in plastic wrap and store in the refrigerator until ready to eat.

Guilt Free Chocolate Soufflé

This recipe makes 6 soufflés' – perfect for entertaining or a special family night treat.

Ingredients

1/4 cup cocoa powder
1/2 cup almond milk
2 Tbsp. coconut flour
6 Tbsp. maple syrup
4 Tbsp. egg whites (or 2 egg whites)
2 tsp vanilla extract

Directions:

Preheat oven to 350 F. In a saucepan over low heat mix cocoa and flour and add milk and the maple syrup.

Heat, stirring for 2 minutes. Stir in vanilla.

In a separate bowl, beat egg whites till stiff peaks form.

Fold about a half of the egg whites into the chocolate mixture. Use a metal spoon to cut the mixture into the chocolate, so you don't remove too much air from the egg whites. Once almost combined, add the other half.

Spoon mixture into ramekin dishes sprayed with cooking oil. You can make six of the size that are pictured here, or four by filling the ramekins a little fuller.

Bake 15 minutes.

SERVE IMMEDIATELY – I typed this in caps as nothing deflates your pride more than a deflated soufflé. Soufflés' have a tendency to sink so keep this one moving as soon as it comes out of the oven.

Calories: 83 and no one will believe the calories are so low

Chocolate Peanut Butter Brownies

Ingredients:

5 egg whites
1.5 scoops chocolate protein powder (we used Trutein Chocolate Peanut Butter Cup)
3/4 cup pumpkin
1/4 cup unsweetened cocoa powder (Hershey's Special Dark works best here)
2 tbsp. coconut flour
2 tbsp. powdered peanut butter + 3 tbsp. for peanut butter swirl (we used PB2)**
1/4 cup mini semi-sweet chocolate chips
1 tsp vanilla
1/2 tsp baking soda
3/4 tsp apple cider vinegar*
Stevia to taste

Directions:

Preheat oven to at 350 and spray a 9 x 9 baking pan with nonstick spray.
In a medium sized bowl, beat egg whites with an electronic mixer for about 30 seconds or until egg whites are foamy, then add all of your wet ingredients and mix well by hand.
Set bowl aside.
In another bowl, combine all dry ingredients except for the chocolate chips.
Slowly add your dry ingredients into your wet ingredients and mix well by hand, then fold in the chocolate chips.
Pour batter into your prepared pan.
To make the peanut butter swirl: In a small bowl add 3 tbsp. of powdered peanut butter and approximately 1.5 tbsp. of water and mix well (you may need more or less water, but you need a slightly "runny" peanut butter for the swirl).
Drizzle the peanut butter over the brownie batter
Then, using a knife gently swirl the batters together. Bake at 350 for 20-25 minutes.
*do not omit as this helps keep the brownies light and fluffy.

Note
You can also substitute real peanut butter for the powdered peanut butter. Just microwave the peanut butter for about 20 seconds to drizzle. Note that this will change the nutritional information.

Calories: 92
Fat: 3.2 g
Carbs: 8.7 g
Fiber: 2.6 g
Protein: 8.7 g
WW Points +: 2 pts

Strawberry Banana Smoothie

I will be the first to admit that strawberry and banana is not my favorite combo but my husband loves this smoothie and I like that we are using fresh fruit so I make it often for him.
I would also recommend this as a great after school treat for kids.

Prep Time: 10 Minutes
Total Time: 10 Minutes

Ingredients

1/2 cup chopped fresh strawberries
1/4 medium banana, peeled and halved
1/4 cup vanilla low calorie nonfat yogurt
1/2 cup crushed ice

Reddi-Wip® Original Dairy Whipped Topping - optional

Directions

Place strawberries, banana and yogurt in blender container.

Pulse until fruit is well blended, scraping sides of container, if necessary.
Add ice; pulse until ice is well blended.
Pour into glass
Optional - top with one serving (2 tablespoons) Reddi-Wip ®.
Serve immediately.

Calories: 84 with whip topping

Strawberry banana smoothies make a great after school treat. Whipped cream is optional – this recipe is great with or without the whipped cream topping.

103 Calorie Chocolate Cupcakes

This treat is a tiny bit over the 100 calorie mark. The cream cheese frosting is a wonderful addition but it will then pull the calories up to 130 total. I have had many compliments on this recipe and due to the response wanted to include it.

Ingredients:

For the cupcakes:
1/2 cup (125 ml) finely grated carrot
2 Tbsp. coconut oil, melted
1 egg
1/2 cup (125 ml) low fat plain yogurt or low fat buttermilk
1 cup minus 2 tbsp. (110g) all -purpose flour
1 tsp baking powder
3/4 tsp baking soda
1/4 tsp salt
1/2 cup (100g) sugar
1/2 cup (50 g) cocoa powder
1/2 cup (125 ml) hot water
For the chocolate cream cheese frosting:
1/2 cup (50g) powdered sugar
1 1/2 Tbsp. cocoa powder
1 1/2 Tbsp. light cream cheese

Instructions:

Preheat your oven to 350 degrees F (180 degrees C).

Put the finely grated carrot into a fine mesh strainer. Hold the strainer over a sink and squeeze the grated carrot to remove as much liquid as possible. Place into a medium bowl.

To the bowl, add the melted oil, egg and yogurt/buttermilk and stir in. Add the next 6 ingredients (flour through to cocoa powder) and stir in. Lastly, stir in the hot water until just combined.

Divide the batter between 12 lined muffin cups. Bake for 20 minutes (or until a toothpick comes out clean). Cool on a wire rack.

For the frosting, combine all the ingredients in a small bowl until smooth. Use about 2 tsp to frost each cupcake.

1 cupcake (without frosting): 103 kcal, 3.3 g fat, 17.5 g carbohydrates (1.1 g fiber, 9.4 g sugars), 2.5 g protein

1 cupcake (with frosting): 128 kcal, 3.7 g fat, 23.0 g carbohydrate (1.3 g fiber, 14.4 g sugars), 2.8 g protein

Apple-Fig Compote

Several years ago I enjoyed a delicious fruit compote at a high end restaurant. When I came across this recipe I thought it would be a beautiful way to end a nice supper at home. Not too heavy but flavorful. The 65 calories per serving was a huge bonus. While I would definitely serve this at the end of fall and winter meals, I think you could also serve during the other seasons.

Total Time: 40 minutes
Prep Time: 15 minutes
Cook Time: 25 minutes

Ingredients

1 lemon
2 pound(s) (4 to 6 medium) Rome Beauty or Jonagold apples, peeled, cored, and cut into 8 wedges
1 1/2 cup(s) apple cider
1 package(s) (8-ounce) dried Calimyrna figs, each cut into quarters
1/2 cup(s) dried tart cherries
1/3 cup(s) sugar
1 stick(s) cinnamon

Directions

From lemon, remove peel with vegetable peeler in 1-inch-wide strips, then squeeze 2 tablespoons juice.

In 4-quart saucepan, combine lemon peel and juice, apples, cider, figs, cherries, sugar, and cinnamon; cover and heat to boiling over high heat. Reduce heat to medium-low; simmer, covered, 20 minutes or until apples are tender, stirring occasionally.

Pour fruit mixture into bowl; serve warm or cover and refrigerate to serve within 4 days.

Nutritional Information
(Per serving)

Calories 65
Total Fat 0
Saturated Fat 0
Cholesterol 0
Sodium 0
Total Carbohydrate 17g
Dietary Fiber 2g
Protein 0

Thank You

Thank you for taking the time to read my book.

Being able to crack the code and find delicious dessert recipes that contained 100 calories or less has made me happy. Being able to share them with others is a great feeling.

As a calorie counter, I am always dumbfounded when I see the insane calorie counts on some desserts. Plus, many times what one would think was a single serving was in fact – 2 or more servings. In essence, thimble size servings.

I have created a Pinterest board www.Pinterest.com/Loera and am compiling more 100 calorie dessert recipes plus a wide variety of other recipes. I hope that if you are on Pinterest and love it as much as I do, that you will follow me.

If you ever need to reach me – loerapublishing@hotmail.com is my email address.

Thank you again for reading my book.

Sincerely,
Diana

Printed in Great Britain
by Amazon